250 PICK U

SUCCESSFUL CHAT UP LII

By Connor Champion

Successful Pick Up Lines

This book will ensure that your pick up routine is a success and that you will never be stuck for ways for approaching someone you fancy.

With 250 pick up lines (some funny, some cheesy, some romantic, some rude; but all successful), you are bound to find many that will suit your personality and will work for you. Armed with this book, your chat up routine will be a huge success and you are going to be on the way to a fun night, romance and maybe even a loving long term relationship.

Acting on the chat up lines in this book will ensure you will have more fun, and more success, than ever before.

Published by Glowworm Press
7 Nuffield Way
Abingdon OX14 1RL

What others have said about this book

"This book has many of the one liners known through the years with a few new ones for good measure. I enjoyed this little book and would encourage any young person entering the dating scene, young meaning 21 and older, to get this book and keep it handy if they want to get lucky."

Mike Williams - Bridgend

"The chat up lines in this book are really good. I have read other books like this where the chat up lines were either really cheesy or I wouldn't dream of trying for fear of getting slapped. A lot of these lines are something I would actually use. I can't wait to try them out. Great Stuff!!"

Graham MacDonald - Dundee

"Not only is this book easy to read, fun and comprehensive - it contains some great lines that will certainly start conversations. Now we just need a follow up book from Connor to help those of us (me I guess) that struggle with responding with any form of wit to the chat up line response... Go on Connor - can you please write "250 witty pick up line response responses to keep the conversation going..."?"

William Hart - Gloucester

Table of Contents

Chapter 1: Introduction

It can be hard to find the right words to say to that one person who has caught your eye. Simply saying "Hello my name is Blah" is lame, and simply will not cut it. For you to be memorable, you will need a great chat up line to break the ice, and to bring a smile to the person you approach.

For you to be memorable and successful, you are going to need some great chat up lines.

In this book you will find the best chat up lines in the world - a staggering 250 chat up lines in total – and they are all winners, and all have proven to be successful

These pick up routines have been field tested in demanding environments - these are successful, proven, battle-tested pick up lines.

We have sorted the pick up lines into the following eight categories:- cheeky, cheesy, corny, flirty, funny, romantic, rude and weird. All of these chat up lines work in different ways and for different reasons.

Here are just a few samples to give you a taste of what to expect in this book:-

In the cheeky chat up line category, we have this gem:- "I'm a great swimmer. Can I demonstrate the breast stroke?" Supporting hand movements are optional.

In the cheesy chat up line category (which is the biggest category) we have:- "Is it hot in here or is it you?"

In the romantic chat up line category you will get to read many sweet chat up lines including:- "I never believed in miracles until I saw you."

There are plenty more waiting you - in fact with 250 pick up lines, you are bound to find many that will suit your personality and will work for you.

Armed with this book, your chat up routine will be a huge success and the first step to a fun night, romance or even a loving long term relationship.

Chapter 2: Cheeky Chat Up Lines

Cheeky chat up lines are brave and slightly saucy without being rude. You will need to be confident and have a cheeky kind of personality to pull these off - these lines will not work if you have a straight face.

- Apart from being sexy, what do you do?

- Are those things real?

- Are we related? Do you want to be?

- Hi, can I buy you several drinks?

- I have lost my teddy bear. Would you sleep with me?

- If I kissed you, would I get slapped?

- If you're going to regret being with me in the morning, we can sleep until noon.

- I'll cook you dinner if you cook me breakfast.

- I'm a doctor and I'm here to offer you a free mammogram.

- I'm a great swimmer. Can I demonstrate the breast stroke?

- I'm feeling a little off today. Would you mind turning me on?

- I may not be a genie, but I can make your dreams come true.

- Is that a mirror in your pocket because I can see myself in your pants?

- One of us is thinking about sex. Okay, it's me.

Chapter 3: Cheesy Chat Up Lines

Cheesy chat up lines are those that you have probably heard before, yet they are proven to work, as they will invariably bring a smile to the girl's face, and that's all you need to get the ball rolling. These are classic openers and are cheesy because they are so over the top.

- Apart from being beautiful, what else do you do?

- Are you accepting applications for your fan club?

- Are your legs tired? Because you have been running through my mind all day.

- Did it hurt? When you fell from heaven.

- Do you have a library card because I'm checking you out!

- Do you have a map? Because I keep getting lost in your eyes.

- Do you mind if I stare at you up close instead of from across the room?

- Here's 10 pence – go phone your mum and tell her you won't be coming home tonight.

- Hey baby, you must be a light switch, because every time I see you, you turn me on!

- I bet your last name is Jacobs - because you're a real cracker!

- I hope you know CPR, because you take my breath away.

- I may not be a genie but I can make your dreams come true.

- I must be in heaven because I can see an angel.

- If I said you had a beautiful body would you hold it against me?

- If this bar were a meat market, you would be the prime rib.

- If you stood in front of a mirror and held up a rose, you would see two of the most beautiful things in the world.

- If you were a hamburger, you'd be a McGorgeous.

- Is it hot in here or is it you?

- Poof! I'm here, what were your other wishes?

- See my friend over there? He wants to know if you think I'm cute.

- Shall we talk or continue flirting from a distance?

- The only thing your eyes haven't told me is your name.

- Was that an earthquake or did you just rock my world?

- Was your dad a King? He must have been to have a princess like you!

- What's a nice girl like you doing talking to someone like me?

- When God made you, he was showing off.

- You know what they say about beauty - it protects against all evil. Well, with you I feel really safe!

- You know, I'm not this tall. I'm just sitting on my wallet.

- You look really hot! You must be the reason for global warming.

Chapter 4: Corny Chat Up Lines

Choose the girl when using any of these corny chat up lines., You have to make sure the girl is the giggly type who doesn't take herself too seriously.

- (Break an ice cube) Now I've broken the ice can I buy you a drink?

- Apart from being beautiful, what do you do for a living?

- Are you a parking ticket because you've got fine written all over you?

- Are you taking any applications for a boyfriend?

- Ask a girl to feel your jumper and then say "What material is that?" She will venture a guess then you say "Boyfriend material."

- Can I take a picture of you? I would like to show Santa what I want for Christmas.

- Can you catch? I am falling for you.

- Do you believe in love at first sight, or should I walk by again?

- Excuse me, but I think I dropped something. My Jaw!

- Excuse me, do you mind if I stare at you for a minute? I want to remember your face for my dreams.

- Fat Penguin! (What?) I just wanted to say something that would break the ice.

- God was just showing off when He made you.

- Here is £20. Drink until I am really good looking, then come back and chat to me.

- Hey baby, I bet you Excel between the spreadsheets.

- Hey, your name is sexy, right?

- Hi, do you speak English? (Yes) Oh, me too.

- How much does a polar bear weigh? Well it's enough to break the ice.

- I don't have a library card, but do you mind if I check you out?

- I guess you can kiss Heaven goodbye. Because it has got to be a sin to look that good.

- I have had a really bad day and it always makes me feel better to see a pretty girl smile. So, would you smile for me?

- Is that a ladder in your tights or is it a stairway to heaven?

- There must be something wrong with my eyes, I can't take them off you.

- I have only three months to live.

- I know I don't have a chance, I just wanted to hear a hottie talk.

- I'm not drunk, I'm just intoxicated by you.

- I'm usually better looking.

- If being sexy was a crime, you'd be guilty as charged!

- I'm invisible. (Really?/No you're not) Well, can you see me? (Yes) How about tomorrow night?

- I'm new in town, could I have directions to your apartment.

- I've been trying to talk to you for ages. No, I still can't do it.

- Life without you would be like a broken pencil - pointless.

- My friend thinks you're hot, and if it's any consolation so do I.

- My love is like an exponential curve. It's unbounded.

- Oh damn I just dropped the keys to my Porsche.

- Someone pass the tartar sauce, because you're quite a catch!

- Sorry I can't talk to you, my doctor told me I'm diabetic and I can't handle sweet things like you.

- There must be something wrong with my eyes; I can't take them off you.

- Were you arrested earlier? It's got to be illegal to look that good.

- You look like the type of girl who's heard every line in the book before, so do you want one more?

- You know something; you really look like my future ex-wife.

- You know, I would die happy if I saw you naked just once!

- You like sleeping? Me too! We should do it together sometime.

- You must be in the wrong place - the Miss World contest is over there.

- You must be Jamaican, because Jamaican me crazy!

- Your Dad must be a thief because he stole the stars and put them in your eyes.

- You're so sweet, you're going to put sugar out of business.

- You're under arrest. The charge – trespassing in my dreams.

Chapter 5: Dirty and Flirty Chat Up lines

These are rude chat up lines but they are also funny, with the emphasis on the fun side. Play on the funny side whilst delivering these lines and you should pull it off.

- *Lick finger and wipe on girl's shirt* Right, let's get you out of those wet clothes.

- Can I add a branch to your family tree?

- Do you sleep on your stomach? If not, can I?

- Do you work for the Post Office? No? I could have sworn I saw you checking out my package.

- F*ck me if I'm wrong, but isn't your name Sylvester?

- Given that god is infinite, and that the universe is also infinite, would you like a shag?

- Hey baby, want to see my elephant?

- How do you like your eggs in the morning – fertilised?

- I don't speak in tongues, but I kiss that way!

- I have a two minute recovery time.

- I may not be the best looking guy here, but I'm the only one talking to you.

- I want to melt in your mouth, not in your hands.

- I'd walk a million miles for one of your smiles, and even farther for that thing you do with your tongue.

- I'm no Fred Flintstone, but I can make your Bedrock!

- Is there a mirror in your knickers? I think I can see myself in them.

- Let's bypass all the bullshit and just get naked.

- Look, just close your eyes and think about George Clooney.

- My name is Carlos. Remember that, you'll be screaming it later.

- Nice dress! Can I talk you out of it?

- Nice dress, it'd look good on my bedroom floor.

- Nice legs. What time do they open?

- One of us is thinking about sex. Okay, it's me.

- Screw me if I'm wrong, but you want to kiss me don't you?

- So, where are we having breakfast?

- Would you like to stroke my lucky scrotum?

- You. Me. Whipped cream. Handcuffs. Any questions?

- Your body reminds me of a spanner. Every time I think of it my nuts tighten up.

- Your Dad must have been a baker, because you've got a nice set of buns.

Chapter 6: Funny Chat Up Lines

These are pick up lines that are meant to make the person laugh - or at worst smile. Hopefully they will do the same for you, so make sure you deliver the lines with a smile.

- Are you religious? (Yes/No) Good, as I am the answer to your prayers.

- Do you believe in helping the homeless? If yes, take me home with you.

- Do you have any raisins? How about a date then?

- Do you know your hair and my pillow are perfectly colour coordinated.

- Get your coat baby; you've just pulled.

- How many camels can I buy you for?

- I'm ready for some FUN, I already have the F and the N, now all I need is U!

- I know Jedi mind tricks. Go home with me tonight you will.

- I suffer from amnesia. Do I come here often?

- I want you to have my children. In fact, you can have them right now, they're out in the car.

- I'm a bird watcher and I'm looking for a Big Breasted Bed Thrasher. Have you seen one?

- Inheriting £10 million doesn't mean much when you have a weak heart.

- Kiss me if I'm wrong, but isn't your name Guadalupe?

- My magical watch says you aren't wearing any underwear! (I am.) It must be an hour fast.

- The voices in my head told me to come over and talk to you

- Want to have sex? Breathe for yes, lick your elbow for no.

Chapter 7: Phone Related Chat Up Lines

In these days of mobile phones and text messaging, your mobile phone can serve as a great prop to help you get the girl. Try some of these on her.

- Can I borrow your mobile phone? I need to phone God and tell him I have found his missing angel.

- I'm doing a survey. What's your name? What's your phone number? Are you free next Saturday?

- I can predict the future - you are going to give me your phone number.

- I don't suppose you know the number for the Ordinance Survey? I want to tell them I have found a sight of outstanding natural beauty.

- I have a pen, you have a phone number. Think of the possibilities.

- I seem to have lost my phone number, can I borrow yours?

- I think there is something wrong with my phone. Could you try calling it for me to see if it rings?

- I'll give you five seconds to give me your number or you can forget going out with me, forever.

- There is something wrong with my mobile. It doesn't have your number in it.

Chapter 8: Romantic Chat Up Lines

These sweet and romantic pick up lines will work best on well mannered, wholesome, sweet and romantic girl next door types.

- Are you a magnet because I'm really attracted to you.

- Are you as beautiful on the inside as you are on the outside.

- Are you religious? Because you are the answer to my prayers.

- Are your lips sore? Here, let me kiss them better.

- Can I have directions? (To where?) To your heart.

- Can you say Constantinople backwards? Me neither, but I just wanted to ask.

- Did the sun come out or did you just smile at me?

- Do you have a map? Because I keep getting lost in your eyes.

- Do you have a quarter/20pence? I told my mum I would call her when I fell in love.

- Have you got a plaster? Because I hurt my knee falling for you.

- Hello, I'm a thief, and I'm here to steal your heart.

- Hi my name's Doug. That's God spelled backwards with a little bit of you wrapped in it.

- How was heaven when you left it?

- I bet I can kiss you on the lips without touching you. [kiss them and tell them you lost the bet.]

- If you were words on a page, you'd be what they call fine print.

- I may be a frog but if you kiss me I may turn into a prince.

- I hope you know CPR? Because you take my breath away.

- I must be lost. I thought paradise was further south.

- I never believed in miracles until I saw you.

- I think you're the light at the end of my tunnel.

- If I could re-arrange the alphabet I would put U and I together.

- If kisses were snowflakes, I'd send you a blizzard.

- If water were beauty, you'd be an ocean.

- I'm like chocolate pudding, I look like crap but I'm as sweet as can be.

- Is there a rainbow nearby, because you're the treasure I've been searching for.

- Is there an airport nearby; or is that just my heart taking off?

- I thought I'd come over and say hello before you caught me staring.

- I've lost that loving feeling. Will you help me find it again?

- Let me tie your shoes, because I don't want you falling for anyone else.

- My friends over there bet that I wouldn't be able to start a conversation with the fittest person in the room. Want to buy some drinks with their money?

- Nice to meet you, I'm (your name) and you are gorgeous!

- There must be something wrong with my eyes; I can't take them off you.

- There's a woman like you in my dreams every night.

- What time do you have to be back in heaven?

- Would you touch me so I can tell my friends I've been touched by an angel?

- You look like my first wife. (Really? How many times have you been married?) None, I'm still a bachelor.

- You must be a hell of a thief because you stole my heart from across the room.

- You plus me equals we.

- You remind me of a compass; because I'd be lost without you.

- You're like a dictionary; you add meaning to my life.

- Your eyes are blue like the ocean and I'm lost at sea.

- Your lips look lonely. Would they like to meet mine?

- Your lips look so sweet, just one kiss and I swear I could give up sugar for life!

- You're hot, I'm cool. Let's get together and even things out.

- You're like a cappuccino: hot, sweet, and you make me nervous.

- You're so hot that when I look at you I get a tan.

Chapter 9: Rude and Crude Chat Up Lines

These pick up lines are lewd, crude and rude - and definitely not suitable if you're a prude.

- Are you a single mother? Would you like to be one?

- Are you an undertaker? Because I have a stiff that needs dealing with urgently.

- Are you doing anything tonight, because I sure hope it is me!

- Are you free tonight, or will it cost me?

- Bad girl! Naughty girl! Go to my room!

- Did you get your jeans on sale? Because in my house they're 100% off.

- Do you have any Irish/Italian/Scottish etc. in you? Would you like some?

- Do you know what a man with a nine inch dick has for breakfast? No? Well I have eggs and bacon!

- Do you know what would look fantastic on you? (No.) Me!

- Do you spit or swallow?

- Do you want to go and do what I'm going to tell my friends we did anyway?

- Do you want to play Army? I will lay down and you can blow the hell outta me.

- Do you want to see something swell?

- Do you work at Subway because you're giving me a foot long.

- Fancy making a porno?

- Hello, I've come about the blow job.

- Hi, my name is {name}, I like peanut butter, wanna f*ck?

- I don't know much about flowers but you can put your tulips around my cock.

- If I'm a pain in your arse, we can just add some lube.

- If you are what you eat, I could be you by morning.

- If you want a carrot, it's yours. If you want 24 carrots, keep on walking lady!

- If you were an ice lolly, I would be licking you all night!

- I like mathematics. You want to go to my room, add the bed, subtract your clothes, divide your legs and multiply?

- I was just curious - are you as good as all the guys say you are?

- I wish you were a door so I could bang you all day long.

- I'm a great shag. Just ask that girl over there.

- I'm an Astronaut. For my next mission, I want to explore Uranus.

- I'd love to see how you look when I'm naked.

- I've just moved you to the top of my 'to do' list.

- I've just received government funding for a four hour expedition to find your G-spot

- Keep it quiet - but I'm completely naked under these clothes.

- Nice shoes. Let's f*ck.

- Sit on my face and tell me that you love me.

- The only thing I want to come between us is latex.

- There are 256 bones in your body! Would you like one more?

- There's a party in my mouth. Do you wanna come?

- Was your father a cement mixer? Because you sure make me hard.

- Were you born on a farm? Because you are very good at raising cocks.

- What has 142 teeth and holds back the Incredible Hulk? The zip in my trousers.

- You may not be the best looking girl here, but beauty is only a light switch away.

- Your name must be Daisy, because I have this incredible urge to plant you right here.

Chapter 10: Weird Chat Up Lines

These pick up lines will sound odd to most people, but if you have a wacky offbeat personality, they may well suit you, and your ability to pull them off.

- Are your parents retarded? Cuz ya sure are special.

- Be unique and different - say yes.

- Did you fart? Cause you just blew me away.

- Excuse me, did you just touch my bum? (No). Damn!

- Hi! I just wanted to give you the satisfaction of turning me down. Go ahead, say No.

- How do you feel about going halves on a bastard?

- I bet you £10 you're going to turn me down.

- I don't know the name of your first, but I'm going to be your last.

- I have many leather bound books, and my apartment smells of rich mahogany.

- If I followed you home, would you keep me?

- If you were a bogey, I would pick you first.

- I'm a Love Pirate, and I'm here for your booty!

- Is that a fox on your shoulder, or am I seeing double?

- I would never, ever videotape you in your sleep and put the video on the Internet.

- I've had quite a bit to drink, and you're beginning to look pretty good.

- My love for you is like diarrhoea. I can't hold it in!

- You sure are ugly, but I bet you feel good in the dark.

- Tickle your pussy with a feather? (What?) I said "Particularly nice weather."

- You don't sweat much for a fat bird!

Chapter 11: Chat Up Lines For Girls

You may be surprised just how much a guy would like a girl to make the first move. It shows that the woman is confident, and there is no doubt that many men find that sexy. Meantime fellas, if you ever get approached by a girl with any of these chat up lines, be sure you have a good answer ready.

- Do these look real to you?

- Do you believe in love at first sight? Or do I have to walk by again?

- Do you have a plaster? I hurt my knee when I fell for you.

- I'm new in town. Could I have the directions to your place?

- I miss my teddy bear. Will you sleep with me?

- I may not be Wilma Flintstone, but I know I can make your Bedrock.

- Is your name Gillette - the best a woman can get?

- Sorry if I'm wrong, but don't you want to kiss me?

- Were you in the Boy Scouts? Because you seem to have tied my heart in a knot.

- You know, honey, my lips won't just kiss themselves.

Chapter 12: The Ten Most Heard Chat Up Lines

These are the lines we heard over and over again, and yes they will all work. You will be pleased to know that in this Top Ten list, some of the pick up lines are cheeky, some are cheesy, some are corny and one is rude.

- Are you tired? Because you've been running through my mind all day.

- Are you a parking ticket, because you've got fine written all over you.

- Did it hurt? When you fell from heaven.

- Do you believe in love at first sight, or should I walk past again?

- Get your coat baby; you've just pulled.

- If I could rearrange the alphabet, I'd put U and I together.

- I have lost my phone number. Can I have yours?

- I hope you know CPR, because you take my breath away.

- I'm no Fred Flintstone, but I can make your Bedrock!

- That dress would look great on my bedroom floor.

Oldies, but Goodies

The author's favourite chat up line which can be used in pretty well all circumstances is:-

"Hi, I'm Mr. Right, someone said you were looking for me."

If all else fails, try this old standby:-

"What's a nice girl like you doing in a place like this?"

Of course, you should never forget the oldest chat up line in the book :-

"Do you come here often?"

About the Author

Connor Champion is a nom de plume for award winning author Carl Christensen; who once started and ran Slow Dating which was for quite a while the UK's favourite speed dating company. He hosted and oversaw many evenings and has seen numerous relationships develop as a result of people using great pick-up lines at speed dating events.

Carl has since written many successful best-selling books.

I hope you enjoyed this book, and if you did, please leave a review on Amazon. Many thanks.